GEARED FOR GROWTH BIBLE STUDIES

COMFORT AND ENCOURAGEMENT

A STUDY IN PSALMS 1–50

BIBLE STUDIES TO IMPACT THE LIVES OF ORDINARY PEOPLE

The Word Worldwide

Written by Rev. Graham Trice

Contents

PREFACE

Welcome to this 'Geared for Growth' Bible Study. It will encourage, challenge and enrich you as you follow it through.

This study is made up of an Introduction and 10 Studies from Psalms 1–50. Easy to read Bible passages indicated for each day are followed by questions to help stimulate a greater understanding of the Bible and encourage positive sharing.

It is strongly recommended that when the studies are used in groups the set daily Bible passages are first read at home and the questions answered by each group member. (Writing the answers down will help in learning). During the group meeting these Bible passages should be reread and answers to the questions shared. The appropriate page of Notes should be read at the end of the study period.

An answer guide is included at the end of this booklet.

Contact the Coordinators on page 55 if you would like help to set up and run a Bible study group. A *Guidelines for Group Leaders* leaflet is also available from the same address.

'Exposing as many people as possible to the truths of God's Word, using Geared for Growth Bible Studies as a tool for evangelism, spiritual growth and the imparting of missionary vision.'

'Where there's LIFE there's GROWTH:
where there's GROWTH there's LIFE.'

WHY GROW a study group?
Because as we study and share the Bible together we can:

- learn to combat loneliness, depression, staleness, frustration and other problems,
- get to understand and love one another,
- become responsive to the Holy Spirit's dealing and obedient to God's Word,

and that's **GROWTH.**

HOW do you **GROW** a study group?

- Just start by asking one friend to join you and then aim at expanding your group.
- Study the set portions daily, they are brief and easy: no catches.
- Meet once a week to discuss what you find.
- Befriend others, both Christians and non-Christians, and work away together.

see how it **GROWS.**

WHEN you GROW...
Things will happen at school, at home, at work, in your youth group, your student fellowship, women's meetings, midweek meetings, churches, communities and so on.

You'll be **REACHING THROUGH TEACHING.**

WHEN you PRAY...
Remember those involved in writing and production of the study courses: for missionaries and nationals working on the translations into many different languages. Pray for groups studying that each member will not only be enriched personally, but will be reaching out continually to involve others. Pray for group leaders and those who direct the studies locally, nationally and internationally.

WHEN you PAY...
Realise that all profits from sales of studies go to develop the ministry on our mission fields and beyond, pay translators and so on, and have the joy of knowing you are working together with them in the task.

INTRODUCTORY STUDY

In that children's classic book *'Alice in Wonderland'* by Lewis Carroll, the King gave the White Rabbit a piece of sound advice about reading. He said, *'Begin at the beginning, and go on till you come to the end: then stop!'* Such sound, practical advice can well be applied to each book of the Bible. The difficulty arises when you come to read and study the longest book in the Bible in a 'Geared for Growth' series. With a total of 150 chapters in the book of Psalms, you really do need more than ten weeks to do the study in! However, we shall partially follow the King's instruction, and we shall begin at the beginning.

DIVIDING THE COLLECTION

It was around one thousand years before the birth of Christ that the Jews divided this large book into five sections. All the Bible quotations in these notes are from the 'New International Version'. If you have a copy you will see that each new section begins with the following *Psalms: 1; 42; 73; 90 and 107.* Just like our chapters and verses these five divisions were made to help the reader, but they were not made under divine inspiration.

QUOTATIONS

I can imagine that the Book of Psalms must surely be the world's most loved, read and quoted collection of poetry in the world. It was certainly the most popular Old Testament book when it came to quotations by the New Testament writers of scripture. Out of approximately 300 direct references made in the New Testament from the Old, it is said that over 100 of these are from the Book of Psalms. Look up the following passages, taking note on whom the quotation is by and to whom it is applied:

Matthew 4:6 (Ps. 91:11, 12), Matthew 7:23 (Ps. 6:8), John 19:24, (Ps. 22:18), Acts 1:20 (Ps. 69:25; 109:8), Romans 2:5 (Ps. 110:5), 2 Timothy 2:14 (Ps. 62:12), Hebrews 5:5, 6, (Ps. 2.7; 110:4).

THE WRITERS

In one hundred of the Psalms the inscription, or title above tells us who the human authors are, while the remaining fifty are anonymous. Who do you think wrote the most? Check the inscription of a small selection such as Psalms 3-9, in case you are in any doubt. An appropriate title is given to this King of Israel in 2 Samuel 23:1, at the end of the verse. The vast majority of the Psalms were composed during his reign. Other valuable contributors to this magnificent collection have lived centuries apart. Discover who wrote the earliest one on the Book of Psalms by turning to the inscription of Psalm 90.

THE STYLE OF THE POETRY

Hebrew poetry does not depend upon rhyme in its composition. It uses thought patterns, and so there is no significant loss of meaning when it is translated. There are three main features which can be found in this book of uplifting poetry.

1. **The use of parallel thoughts.** Double statements are often made, with the second one amplifying the first. Look at Psalms 1 and 2 for examples of this.
2. **The use of images.** One thing is used to represent another. What are the images used to represent restless people and nations in Psalm 93:3, 4?
3. **The use of the alphabet.** The letters are sometimes ordered for the first word in each verse or section of the Psalm. The best example of this is Psalm 119; even in our English translation the Hebrews letters are used.

GROUP TITLES

A wide variety of suggestions have been made as to how to classify the many different types of Psalm. These are just a few examples of suggested descriptive titles for groups of Psalms: Teaching; Historical; Prophetic; Sorrowful; Praising; Morning; Evening; Messianic (that is, they include predictions that refer to the Lord Jesus Christ). See if you can allocate one of the Psalms to each of the above titles: Psalm 1; 4; 5; 22; 78; 97; 150.

THE RANGE OF TOPICS

There is hardly a human experience or spiritual condition that is not dealt with in this amazing and versatile book. Topics such as grief, doubt, oppression, anxiety, death, repentance, restoration, joy, thankfulness and praise are dealt with. There is an outstanding variety of issues that are dealt with in a beneficial manner. How can there not be something especially for you with such a diverse range of topics covered?

A PRAYER

'May the words of my mouth
And the meditation of my heart
Be pleasing in your sight,
O Lord, my Rock and my Redeemer,'
Psalm 19:14.

HELPFUL BOOKS ON THE PSALMS

'Of making many books there is no end, and much study wearies the body...' Ecclesiastes 12:12b, So wrote the wise King Solomon centuries ago. How true his words have proved to be! There are a vast amount of books written to help us understand the Book of Psalms in the Bible. From the vast array of good books, excellent authors and Christian publishers, here is a small selection which you should be aware of:

Psalms, Volume I, Psalms 1-50, Songs of Devotion, by Robert L. Alden
(Moody Press, ISBN-978-0-80242-018-3). This easy to read and understand little paper back is the one recommended for use with this study. The publisher kindly granted permission for quotations to be used in these notes.

Psalms 1-72, An Introduction and Commentary, by Derek Kidner.
(Inter-Varsity Press, ISBN 978-0-85111-828-4). This is in the Tyndale Old Testament series. It is brief but more technical than Robert Alden's book, it is nevertheless a valuable study tool.

The Treasury of David, by Charles Haddon Spurgeon.
The unabridged edition is in several volumes. It is definitely for the serious reader and keen Bible student, but as the name suggests, it is a spiritual treasure chest, packed full of precious gems.

John Calvin, Matthew Henry and Matthew Poole are some of the great writers of the past whose excellent writings are still being published today, often in sets. They provide the mature Christian reader with a lot to read and think about.

STUDY 1

PSALMS 1-6

QUESTIONS

DAY 1 The Saint and the Sinner. *Psalm 1; Jeremiah 17:5-8.*

a) What two types of people are described in the Psalm?

b) Using words from the Psalm, find a statement that best describes your life?

DAY 2 The King of Kings. *Psalm 2:1-6; Acts 4:25, 26.*

a) Find two special titles that refer to the Lord Jesus Christ?

b) Who are in revolt against the Lord (vv. 1-3)?

c) What is God's reaction to this (vv. 4-6)?

DAY 3 The Conquest of Christ. *Psalm 2:7-12; Revelation 5:9, 10.*

a) Can you find another of Christ's special titles from verses 7 and 12?

b) How far should we expect Christ's conquest to spread (v. 8)?

c) What important lessons can be drawn from the Psalm's last verse?

DAY 4 A Morning Psalm. *Psalm 3; 2 Samuel 15:11-14.*

a) Have you ever lain down to sleep feeling anxious, sad or concerned about your family, and wondered what the next day would be like?

b) How did David get the help he needed in his time of trouble (vv. 4-6)?

DAY 5 An Evening Psalm. *Psalm 4; Acts 12:6, 7.*

a) What makes it possible for me to 'sleep in peace,' like David and like Peter who was 'asleep in prison' the night before a trial?

DAY 6 The Praying Poet. *Psalm 5.*

a) How did David begin his day?

b) How do you begin your day?

c) What does David ask in prayer for those who trust the Lord (v. 11)?

DAY 7 Sorrowing over Sin. *Psalm 6; 2 Corinthians 7:10; 1 John 1:9.*

a) Was the sorrow of the Psalmist 'godly' or 'worldly'?

b) Discuss. Is it enough just to be sorry for our sins?

NOTES

Psalm 1

"Like a tree by a river" - what does the Psalmist mean?

a) Strong and steady - not swayed by any new doctrine, but rooted and grounded in faith.
b) Drawing in nourishment all the time - delighting in the Word, thinking it through, letting it reach our inmost parts.
c) Staying fresh and green - alert to what God is saying to us, and putting it into action.
d) Producing fruit - showing forth Christ in our lives and sharing his truth with others.

Psalm 2

The big powers meet for summit talks.

'All we need is careful negotiation and a majority vote. We don't need God.'

But God laughs! ...and then he is angry.

'There is only one King, and He is my Son. I have the perfect plan for the world and it includes people from every tribe and nation who will worship and serve Me.'

Psalm 3

Absalom has seized the throne.

Quick, we must get out of Jerusalem! The people who were once my subjects have become my enemies - led by my own son. O God help! Hurry, men, hurry!

And God does help. He takes away David's fear, replaces it with peace, and with the assurance that God will help him.

Psalm 4

A missionary couple who were working in West Africa had an alarming experience one evening. A few minutes after taking their daughter out of her cot, they discovered a long snake beneath it. Later that evening when the couple sat down for their regular time of Bible reading and prayer, they were still concerned about the family's safety. In the remarkable providence of God they had reached Psalm 4 in their systematic reading of the Scriptures. What a blessing and comfort the final verse of this psalm proved to be on that memorable evening!

Psalm 5

What a delightful pattern for the days we have here.

Morning: Time to talk to the Lord, pour out your heart, bring your requests. Wait in expectation.

Throughout the day: Pray that the Lord will lead you in his perfect way, and show clearly the way ahead.
The result: Gladness, joy, protection and blessing.

Psalm 6
This is surely the heart-cry of a man who is conscious of his sin, sick in body, and utterly miserable. How would we expect God to respond? Does he really care when we are suffering? What would a human father do? He would take the child in his arms and comfort him.

And God is ready to do just that.

"The Lord has heard my weeping,
The Lord has heard my cry for mercy,
The Lord accepts my prayer."

Be encouraged! If you are suffering physically, or emotionally, or because of sin, let God the Father hear your cry. He is waiting to take you in his arms.

STUDY 2

PSALMS 7-11

QUESTIONS

DAY 1 The Slandered Saint. *Psalm 7:1-9.*

a) How did David react to the slander of Cush?

He prayed for God's justice

b) What do the words, 'O Lord my God' (vv. 1, 3) reveal about David's prayer and his relationship with God?

DAY 2 The Slandered Saint. *Psalm 7:10-17; Matthew 5:11, 12.*

a) How do you respond to false accusations?

Calmly - clarify situations ABCD
3rd party - anger

b) What can we learn about the way God sometimes deals with the unrighteous trouble maker?

God always judges, trouble backfires on the individual.

DAY 3 The Dignity of Man. *Psalm 8; 1 Corinthians 15:27; Hebrews 2:6-8.*

a) When the New Testament writers quoted from this Psalm, to whom did they apply the passages? Jesus

written To Christians in Corinth
+ To converted Hebrews (Jewish) Christians in Jerusalem

b) Discuss what can be done today to encourage a greater respect for human dignity?

All men have been given this great place in our world.

DAY 4 God's Righteous Judgement. *Psalm 9:1-12; Genesis 18:25.*

a) How does the Psalmist express his praise to God?

with all his heart

b) How do you equate praise and God's punishment in this psalm?

Comfort - that those who sin will be punished. This is something to give praise for.

c) Read again God's purposes in verses 7-12. Which verses encourage you?

9 The Lord is a refuge for the oppressed, a stronghold in times of trouble.
10. You have never forsaken those who seek you.
12 God does not ignore the cry of the afflicted.

DAY 5 The Reigning and Righteous Judge. *Psalm 9:13-20.*

a) What phrases in the Psalm show that God is both the Reigning and Righteous Judge?

v7 The Lord reigns forever, he has established his throne for judgement; he will judge in righteousness

b) Who should be fearful of this fact and who should be thankful?

19-20 The nations
16 The wicked

9. The oppressed
10. Those who know your name.
12 The afflicted.
18 The needy

DAY 6 The Prayer of a Persecuted Man. *Psalm 10; Exodus 3:7, 8.*

a) Why are we sometimes tempted to ask God, 'Why...?' (vv. 1, 13).

b) How did the Psalmist answer his own question and console himself? (v14).

God does see + takes it in hand.

DAY 7 The Refuge of the Righteous. *Psalm 11; 46:1.*

a) Is God your eternal Refuge? Can you honestly say with the preacher and hymn writer Charles Wesley, 'Other refuge have I none...?'

b) Discuss how you came to seek refuge in the Lord?

NOTES

Psalm 7

Who is this man, "Cush, a Benjamite," who is spoken of in the psalmist's inscription?

We cannot definitely say, as he is not mentioned anywhere else in the Bible. However, we know that many of David's enemies came from the tribe of Benjamin. There were three in particular:

> **Saul** (1 Sam. 9:1, 2). The first King of Israel who attempted to kill David on several occasions.
> **Shemei** (2 Sam. 16:5-7). He cursed David even as he fled for his life at the time of Absalom's conspiracy.
> **Seba** (2 Sam. 20:1). This man is described as a 'troublemaker'.

It has been said that, "Sticks and stones can break my bones; but names will never hurt me!" Many of us, including David (I think), would want to disagree with such sentiments, because we do feel hurt when we are falsely accused. The question arises, "What are we to do as Christians if we are slandered?" We could try following a formula such as this ABCD one based upon Psalm 7.

> **A**sk for God's help first of all (vv. 1-2).
> **B**e prepared to examine your own life (vv. 3-5).
> **C**omfort yourself with the fact that God is Just (vv. 6-16).
> **D**on't stop praising the Lord (v. 17).

Psalm 8

When astronaut John Glenn travelled out into space, he quoted this psalm. As he considered the heavens, he marvelled at the work of God's fingers, his glory set above the heavens. And, looking down at that tiny ball called earth, suspended in the night sky, he could only stand amazed that the Creator should care about those infinitesimally small human creatures on it.

David, writing this psalm, had similar thoughts - but notice that this was even before the Creator's Son had visited planet earth! From the beginning of time, God endowed mankind with a special dignity that pointed to his eternal destiny.

Psalm 9

What an incredible statement of faith David made when he confidently wrote, "God will judge the world in righteousness"! How could he know that? He couldn't prove it. It didn't always appear to be happening. As he says in another psalm, *"The wicked are always carefree, they increase in wealth."*

Don't you agree that it often looks as though the wicked get away with their wrongdoing?

But God revealed to David the eternal truth that he is King and Judge and that ultimately the wicked will be punished. What a glorious truth! It is enough to make us sing praises to God! He is the righteous judge.

To believe this requires an incredible faith... in an incredible God.

Psalm 10

Here we have a portrait of a wicked person. What did you notice about him?

He is crafty and plans schemes to demoralise the weak.
He is proud and boasts that nothing can topple him.
He has no room for God, indeed he says, "God is dead".
He curses, tells lies and threatens others.
He is a murderer, confident that he will never be found out.

Doesn't this description make you think of Satan, who is, in fact, behind every evil in the world?

David is impatient that God doesn't act more quickly, but eventually realises that God has everything in hand and will give punishment when the time is right.

Psalm 11

The Lord is in his holy temple.
The Lord is on his heavenly throne.
The Lord examines the righteous.
The Lord is righteous and loves justice.

David had a clear conscience, so where else would he go to find refuge from his enemies, but to the Lord? His friends had other ideas. "Run away and hide," they advised, "Your world is crumbling around you, you'll never survive."

David knew that God was in control. He trusted his God in times of trouble. We must prove God is faithful when we are faced with problems.

STUDY 3

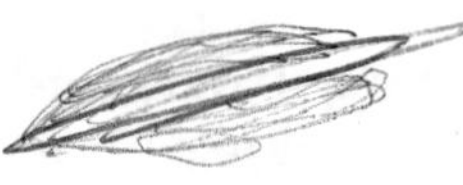

PSALMS 12-17

QUESTIONS

DAY 1 Terrible Times. *Psalm 12:2; 2 Timothy 3:1-5.*
"The heart is deceitful above all things..." (Jer. 17:9).

a) What words tell of the absence of the following in the natural human heart, (vv. 2, 8)?

Lies, deception, vileness

b) How many features in Paul's 'terrible times' list can you identify as being present in today's society?

Lies, oppression needy, deception, vileness

c) What ought we to do in such times?

Pray

DAY 2 From Sorrow to Song. *Psalm 13.*

a) What was it that caused you to ask, 'How long O Lord?'

b) How was David able to move on from his state of turmoil and frustration?

Trusting in God's unfailing love.

DAY 3 The Folly of Fools. *Psalm 14; 1 Corinthians 4:10; Psalm 92:6.*

a) What sort of fool was the Apostle Paul?

A fool for Christ

b) Can you name another person who is called a fool in the Bible? (A concordance may be useful).

DAY 4 David's Catechism. *Psalm 15; Hebrews 12:25-29; Psalm 16:5.*

a) How many points are raised in the answer to David's questions, (vv. 2-5)?

b) Which of these do you find the hardest to practice?

c) Who are those who will not be shaken?

DAY 5 Deliverance from Death. *Psalm 16; Acts 2:25-32; 13:35-37.*

a) What enabled David to be personally assured about his death?

b) Who were the New Testament speakers and to whom did they apply the text from Psalm 16?

DAY 6 The Requests of the Righteous. *Psalm 17:1-7; James 5:16; Psalm 66:17-20.*

a) If our prayers are to be 'powerful and effective', what must we do?

b) To what extent does David's 'self-portrait' in these verses describe you?

DAY 7 Praying for Protection. *Psalm 17:8-15; Romans 15:30-32.*

a) Write out David and Paul's needs for prayer?

b) Share your prayer needs.

c) Pray for each others needs.

NOTES

Psalm 12

Do you ever feel depressed because you are the only Christian in your work place, or university group, or among your relatives? Are you sickened by filthy language, dirty jokes and suggestive comments you hear day after day?

That's just how David felt as he poured out his heart to God. (What a good thing to do!) Then he discovered a wonderful contrast between the lies spoken by those around him, and the words of the Lord which are flawless and pure as silver.

Psalm 13

Have you ever experienced the sense of confusion and frustration that David is expressing at the beginning of this psalm? He could not always understand God's purpose in keeping him waiting. It's so easy to feel impatient with God and want things to happen right away. However, notice that even in his confusion David continued to pray, and eventually he was able to rejoice and sing. You could write out verses 5 and 6 and use them often in your time alone with God.

Psalm 14

Here is a picture of a seeking God looking down from heaven to find people who love him. This theme occurs throughout the Bible:

- The Lord saw how great man's wickedness on earth had become...but Noah found favour in the eyes of the Lord, (Gen. 6:5, 8).
- The eyes of the Lord range throughout the earth to strengthen those whose hearts are fully committed to him, (2 Chron. 16:9).
- True worshippers will worship the Father in spirit and truth, for they are the kind of worshippers the Father seeks, (John 4:23). And he is still seeking.

David concludes the psalm with the assurance that God will restore the fortunes of those who love him, and there will be rejoicing.

Psalm 15

Eugene Peterson, in *The Message*, opens this psalm with these words:

> "God, who gets invited to dinner at Your place?
> How do we get on Your guest list?"

David gives us a lot of do's and don'ts that read rather like the Ten Commandments. A high ideal - but who can keep them all? Alongside this psalm we must put the words of Jesus:

> "I am the Way, the Truth and the Life.
> No man comes to the Father except by Me."

Only when he has clothed us in his righteousness can we have that blameless walk that will make us eligible to sit at his table.

Psalm 16

This psalm exudes confidence - confidence in God.

Although David writes psalms when he is in all types of different moods, here he is as steady as a rock. When things are going well we too need to remember to praise God for:

His protection,
The eternal security we have in him,
our glorious inheritance in the saints,
his counsel and guidance,
the joy of his presence,
and the hope of heaven.

Are you confident on your path of life? Praying these verses often will help you to become as steady as a rock.

Psalm 17

When you read 1 Samuel, you discover that many times Saul thought he had David cornered. At such times David prayed prayers like this psalm.

When David was told the Philistines were fighting against Keilah, he wanted to help - but was he making himself a sitting duck for Saul?

In 1 Samuel 23:2 we read that, *he enquired of the Lord saying, "Shall I go and attack these Philistines?" The Lord answered him, "Go, attack the Philistines and save Keilah."*

Again we see David enquiring of the Lord in 1 Samuel 23:4; and in verses 10-12 we read how David asked the question, *"O Lord, God of Israel ...will Saul come down?...will the citizens of Keilah surrender me to him? And the Lord said, "He will."*

Again David asked, "Will the citizens of Keilah surrender me and my men to Saul?" And the Lord said, "They will."

To read, "he enquired of the Lord", may sound unemotional and prosaic, but Psalm 17 opens a window onto his feelings. It is a passionate plea of a man, unjustly hounded by the king, yet clinging desperately to his only hope - the Lord.

And the result?

1 Samuel 23:14. *David stayed in the desert strongholds and in the hills of the Desert of Ziph. Day after day Saul searched for him, but God did not give David into his hands.*

I was overcome by trouble and sorrow, then I called on the name of the Lord Save me! Ps 116:3,4

If the Lord had not been on ours when men attack the raging water would have swept all away. Ps 124:2

STUDY 4

PSALMS 18-23

QUESTIONS

DAY 1 David's Song of Deliverance. *Psalm 18:1-24; 116:3, 4; 124:2, 5.*

a) Suggest reasons for all the personal pronouns such as 'I' and 'my' being used in these verses.

He is greatful for his life, safety after all he's been through - danger

b) When great trials of life are against you, what do you do?

DAY 2 David's Triumphant Testimony. *Psalm 18:25-50.*

a) Who turned David's darkness into light?

The Lord

b) Who was given the 'shield of victory'?

DAVID

c) Who cried to the Lord in vain?

David's enemies

DAY 3 Divine Revelation. *Psalm 19; Romans 1:18-20.*

a) How does God make himself known through creation and His Word?

The Heavens + the skies
His Law

b) How does God's Word benefit us personally as described in verses 7-11?

- they give wisdom + living by them gives joy.

The sky varied, changing, heavy, high, moving, light, blue, grey, bright

DAY 4 Requests before the Battle. *Psalm 20; 1 Timothy 2:1, 2.*

a) Which verses denote a great sense of anticipation that God will hear and answer prayer?

5 - we will shout for Joy   7 we trust in the name of the Lord
6. I know the Lord saves.

b) Do you always anticipate that God will answer your prayers?

Yes, but maybe not in the way I think.

c) Suggest people 'in authority' for whom we should pray?

Queen, Government, teachers

DAY 5 Rejoicing after the Battle. *Psalm 21; 2 Peter 3:10-12.*

a) Do you have cause to exclaim, 'How great is my joy in the victories you give!? Can you give a past or present example?

Battles?

b) What implications are revealed in *verse* 9 in the light of *2 Peter 3:10-12?*

God's wrath will be displayed in a mighty fire

DAY 6 The Song about Suffering. *Psalm 22.*

a) Note how David alternates between apparently complaining and trusting in verses 1-21?

b) When do you find yourself doing the same thing?

DAY 7 The Personal Shepherd. *Psalm 23; John 10:11.*

a) When does the 'Good Shepherd' become 'my Shepherd'?

b) Can you recite the psalm from memory? If not, make the effort to do so.

NOTES

Psalm 18

Miraculous deliverances have frequently been a stimulus to praise the Lord. For example, the song sung by Moses and Miriam after the Israelite deliverance from slavery in Egypt (Exod. 15), Deborah and Barak's song following the defeat of Sisera and his powerful army (Judg. 5). In 2 Samuel 22:1 we read, *'David sang to the Lord the words of this song, when the Lord delivered him from the hand of his enemies and from the hand of Saul.'* Then came the words of this psalm. Thus, what was first written in a historical book of the Bible, is now set before us in a poetical book.

See the long inscription of Psalm 18.

The song was written towards the end of David's life, so he was able to look back over many trials. Now, in a spirit of praise and worship, he can testify to the Lord's gracious deliverance 'from all his enemies'.

Psalm 19

A poet once wrote:

> "What is this life if, full of care,
> We have no time to stand and stare?"

Think about it.
Stop right now and look up, outside. What are the heavens - the skies - saying to you about God? How tragic if we should miss these heavenly messages!

In this psalm, David informs us about ways in which God makes himself known to mankind:

1. **God's Natural Revelation** in the sky (vv. 1-6).
   C.H.Spurgeon has said that the "sun, moon and stars are God's travelling preachers" (Rom. 1:20).

2. **God's Spiritual Revelation** through the Scriptures (vv. 7-11).
   The inspired and infallible Word of God, the Bible, is God's supreme way of revealing himself to us. The Scriptures inform us all that we need to know about him.

3. **God's Personal Revelation** to our soul's (vv. 12-14).
   David testifies about the effect of God's revelation upon him. Notice how it began with conviction (v. 12), and then led to intercession (vv. 13-14a) and adoration (v. 14b).

Psalm 20 and 21
"God save the King!" (20:9).

20:5	We shall shout for the joy when you are victorious.
21:1	How great is his joy in the victories you give.
20:4	May he give you the desires of your heart.
21:2	You have granted him the desires of your heart.
20:7	We trust in the name of the Lord our God.
21:7	For the King trusts in the Lord.
20:8	We will rise up and stand firm.
21:7	He will not be shaken.
20:8	They are brought to their knees and fall.
21:8	Your hand will lay hold on all your enemies.

These two psalms remind us that we can share every situation with the Lord. Read Psalm 21 again, applying it to the Lord Jesus.

Psalm 22
In Matthew 27:46 we are told that Jesus cried out to God with the opening words of this psalm. Jesus would have known the psalms by heart, and verses 6-10 must also have been in his mind. Yet the most horrific aspect of the crucifixion was that in order to bear the sins of the world, he had actually to be forsaken by His Father.

David could pray 'deliver my life' (v. 20), and the chief priests could mock, 'let God deliver him' (Matt. 27:43), but for Jesus there was no deliverance. He drank the cup of suffering to its dregs.

Only then could he utter the words with which this psalm closes, 'He has done it' – in the Greek, 'It is finished!'

Psalm 23
This is surely the most read, sung, recited and loved psalm of the 150 in the collection! The simple picture language reveals God's loving care for all those who are his sheep. C.H.Spurgeon has sounded this appropriate warning, 'No man has a right to consider himself the Lord's sheep unless his nature has been renewed, for the spiritual description of the unconverted men does not picture them as sheep, but as wolves and goats'.

STUDY 5

PSALMS 24-30

QUESTIONS

DAY 1 **'The King of Glory'.** *Psalm 24; Acts 1:9-11; John 17:24.*

a) What is required of worshippers in God's holy presence?

b) For whom did the King of King's pray that they would see his glory?

DAY 2 **Please Pardon and Protect.** *Psalm 25.*

a) When did you last use phrases such as *'forgive my iniquity,' 'take away all my sins'* in prayer?

b) Who did David ask to help and protect him? Share when you most sense your need to do this?

c) In what ways did David ask for help and protection?

DAY 3 **God's House - A Place of Searching.** *Psalm 26; 1 Chronicles 29:17; Psalm 139:23, 24.*

a) David said, *'I know my God that you test the heart...'* Compare this with verse 2 and discuss how this takes place.

Testing the heart?

very beautiful

b) What was the affirmation David made when ending this psalm?

I will praise the Lord.

DAY 4 God's House - A Place of Safety. *Psalm 23:6; Psalm 27:1-6.*

a) How was it possible for David to speak with such assurance and say, '*I will dwell in the house of the Lord forever.' and '...He will keep me safe in his dwelling'*?

His experience of God, answered prayer.

b) How can we have a similar assurance?

through the Holy Spirit

DAY 5 God's House - A Place of Safety. *Psalm 27:7-14.*

a) Discuss the possible outcome of praying, '*Teach me your way...*'

It might not be our way.

b) What is the repeated instruction in the final verse?

Wait for the Lord - His timing might not be ours.

DAY 6 God's House - A Place of Supplication. *Psalm 28; 1 Timothy 2:8.*

a) Compare David's words in verse 2 with Paul's words in 1 Timothy 2:8 and discuss how this might apply to us today?

b) What effect does my praise to God have in my worship?

Takes focus off my problems

DAY 7 The Voice of the Lord. *Psalm 29.*

a) What are the duties which David highlights at the commencement of this psalm?

b) What can we learn about the Lord from what we are told about his voice?

Power, Majesty, Frightening

NOTES

Psalm 24

What joyful praise and thanksgiving is expressed in this lovely song! We can only speculate about the occasion in David's reign for which it was originally written. Yet in our imagination we can surely see the real King of glory entering the celestial gates at His ascension, with ten thousand times ten thousand angels singing,

"Worthy is the Lamb who was slain, to receive glory and praise!"

This theme has been taken up by several Christian hymn writers:

Hail the day that sees him rise,
Glorious to his native skies;
Christ, awhile to mortals given,
Enters now the highest heaven.

There the glorious triumph waits;
Lift your heads, eternal gates!
Christ hath vanquished death and sin;
Take the king of glory in!

Charles Wesley (1707-88) altered by Thomas Cotterill (1779-1823)

Glory, glory to our King!
Crowns unfading wreathe His head.
Jesus is the name we sing,
Jesus risen from the dead,
Jesus conqueror o'er the grave,
Jesus mighty now to save.

Jesus is gone up on high;
Angels come to meet their King;
Shouts triumphant rend the sky,
While the victors praise we sing:
Open now ye heavenly gates!
'Tis the King of glory waits.

Thomas Kelly (1769-1854).

Psalm 25

If I knew what God's will was for my life, I'd gladly do it. But how can I know? Is this your problem?

Do you think David expected God to show him His ways? (v. 4). Did he expect Him to guide and teach him? (v. 5). To show him what was right? (v. 9). And to instruct him in the way chosen for him? (v. 12).
He must have done.

And you too can expect God to show you, when you ask him.
However... there are conditions.

1. Complete trust in God.

2. Repentance and forgiveness.

Psalm 26

'Test me, o God, and try me.'

The final verses of psalm 139 come to mind when reading this prayer of David. Can you honestly ask God to test you and examine you? He knows all about you, anyway!

Most of this psalm reads as if David was boasting about his own righteous life, but as we look deeper we see that he is merely stating his determination to please the Lord in everything. His humility comes out in verse 11 when he asks God for mercy.

Psalm 27

Can you sense the excitement of this psalm? Every verse thrills with David's delight in the Lord who is his hiding-place, his protector, and the answer to his deepest longing.

Ask the Lord to help you to get more excited about Him. Then consider each of these superb verses one at a time and use them when praising Him.

Psalm 28

Joseph Scriven's hymn which begins, 'What a Friend we have in Jesus', goes on to say, 'What a privilege to carry *everything* to God in prayer!' In this short psalm David appears to be taking full advantage of this privilege. He appeals to the Lord to hear and help him. He prays against the desires of evil men. He remembers to give God praise and thanks, and he also prays for others. Before he concludes his prayer it is as if Isaiah 65:24 has become a reality to him: *"Before they call, I will answer. While they are still speaking, I will hear."*

Psalm 29

Some see in this psalm the song of a thunderstorm on earth viewed from the courts of heaven.

v. 1, 2	The heavenly scene with the angels summoned to join in the praise and worship of the Lord.
v. 3	The storm approaches from the west over the waters of the Mediterranean, gathering its tremendous energy.
vv. 4-6	It passes across the forested hills of Lebanon and Mount Hermon in a wild, exuberant dance.
vv. 7-9	It continues to be cast over the desert, leaving behind a trail of uprooted trees and shattered branches.
vv. 10, 11	In total contrast, the Lord sits calmly watching the display of His power, while the heavenly hosts shout His praise.

STUDY 6

PSALMS 30-34

QUESTIONS

DAY 1 Thank You Lord! *Psalm 30; 1 Corinthians 10:12, 13.*

a) David may be confessing his former sins of presumption and self confidence in verse 6. When have you yielded to that temptation?

b) Who was fully responsible for David's healing and deliverance?

c) What was David's response?

DAY 2 A Saint under Stress. *Psalm 31:1-13.*

a) What positive statement did David pray back to the Lord?

b) Link the following references to phrases from the psalm: *Psalm 71:14; Luke 23:46; Acts 7.59; Jonah 2:8; Jeremiah 6:25; 20:10; 46:5; 49:5 and Lamentations 2:22.*

DAY 3 A Saint who is Strengthened. *Psalm 31:14-24; 2 Corinthians 1:4.*

a) In his state of alarm, what did David first say when finding himself in great difficulty?

b) Discuss the times when God seemed far away.

c) What was the beneficial outcome that followed David's time of stress?

DAY 4 Features of Forgiveness. *Psalm 32.*

a) When David was silent about his sin, what effect did it have upon him?

Bones wasted, felt the hand of God heavy upon him strength sapped as in summer's heat.

b) What was the outcome when David confessed his sin?

God forgave him

c) Who are being encouraged to rejoice and sing?

those who trust the Lord

DAY 5 Our Maker and Monarch. *Psalm 33; Hebrews 1:10; 11:33.*

a) Discuss how the psalmist's comments about the creation differ from the popular opinions of today.

b) Why should we, '*sing* joyfully *to the Lord*'?

DAY 6 Rejoicing with David. *Psalm 34:1-10.*

a) Suggest ways of applying and using verses 1-3.

John Ortberg -

b) When the Lord saved David how did he express his thankfulness?

In Praise

c) In what other ways does God protect his children?

DAY 7 Listening to David. *Psalm 34:11-22; Romans 8:1.*

a) What do we learn about the eyes, ears and face of the Lord in this section of the psalm?

The eyes of the Lord are on the righteous, his ears are attentive to their cry. The face of the Lord is against those who do evil. The Lord hears the righteous

b) What important lesson is being taught by David and Paul in our readings?

c) What assurance does the Word of God give us when we feel condemned?

We should take refuge in the Lord.

NOTES

Psalm 30

Mourning and dancing - could any two experiences be in greater contrast?

Mourning	Dancing
in the depths	you lifted me up
enemies waiting to gloat	you restrained the enemies
call for help	you healed me
going down to the grave	you spared me
weeping in the night	joy in the morning
I cried for mercy	you turned sorrow into joy

No wonder David rejoiced and sang to God for his goodness!

Psalm 31

Stress-related illness is no new thing. David was a man who was frequently under stress and of necessity had to look to the Lord for help. In a very humble manner David exposes to us his own human weakness in this psalm and thus we gain an insight into a godly man under stress.

It is interesting to note that both Old and New Testament saints have quoted or alluded to phrases in this psalm when they were under great stress themselves. We should also note that having to pass through a stressful period David was stimulated to pray earnestly about the problem. He admitted his own weakness, yet at the same time looked to God for strength and was able to praise God for his 'wonderful love'.

Psalm 32

What great advice David gives us here!

'Confess your sin, don't cover it up.'

And the result? Forgiveness and the removal of guilt. That's why Jesus died, so that we can be forgiven and our guilt be taken right away. Isn't it wonderful that the Holy Spirit inspired David to write this so long before Jesus came?

Verse 8 is a promise we can claim when our transgressions are forgiven and our sins are covered.

Psalm 33

Keep in mind that the psalms are pure poetry. This one almost sings as we read it, and indeed we find that God loves to hear us praising Him on all kinds of musical instruments.

Majestic pictures of God appear in these verses:
He spoke the world into existence,
He foils the plans of nations,
He looks down and sees all mankind,
He cares for His people.
Our response should be:
to wait,
to trust,
to hope in him.

Psalm 34
David was really in a tight spot.
Pursued by Saul and his soldiers, he fled to Philistine country to seek shelter. But the servants of King Achish recognised him, and to save his skin he pretended to be mad (I Sam. 21:10-15).

After he had escaped from there he wrote this psalm, praising God for his deliverance.

What had God done?
He answered him,
He delivered him,
He heard him,
He saved him

There are many beautiful verses in this psalm. It would be good to memorise them.

STUDY 7

PSALMS 35-38

QUESTIONS

DAY 1 The Fierce Conflict. *Psalm 35:1-18; 34:7; 2 Kings 19:35; Matthew 5:43, 44.*

a) Discuss the work of the 'angel of the Lord' as spoken of in the psalm (vv. 5, 6).

Scary picture.

b) Contrast David's words in this section of the psalm with Christ's words to his disciples in Matthew 5.

He is fearful, loving his enemies is far from his mind. 35:19-28

DAY 2 The False Charges. *Psalm 35:18, 19; I Kings 21:13; Matthew 26:59, 60a; Acts 6:13, 14; 24:12, 13.*

a) Name others who had to contend with false accusations'.

Naboth, Paul, Stephen, Jesus.

b) Together with David, what did all these people have in common?

They loved the Lord.

c) How do you deal with false accusations?

Hurt, angry

DAY 3 Man's Wickedness and God's Worthiness. *Psalm 36; Romans 3:9-18.*

a) Compare David's words in verses 1-4 with Paul's.

Wicked, deceitful

b) Summarise mankind's condition as described by these two men of God.

c) List the characteristics of God that are mentioned in the psalm.

God's love
faithfulness
righteousness
Justice

DAY 4 A Message for all Mankind. *Psalm 37:1-17.*

a) Which ones from David's list of 'recommendations' in verses 1-9 have you actively sought to put into practice?

Do not fret - it leads only to evil
Be still before the Lord + wait patiently.

b) Which do you find the most difficult to comply with consistently?

Be still
Refrain from anger

DAY 5 Condemnation or Salvation? *Psalm 37:18-40.*

a) What are the future prospects of the unconverted (vv 20, 35-36, 38) and the righteous (vv. 37, 39-40)?

The wicked will perish but the Lord saves the righteous-

b) List the spiritual prospects of the righteous?

our inheritance will last forever

DAY 6 A Cry for Compassion. *Psalm 38:1-12; Luke 10:30-37; 2 Chronicles 28:15.*

a) How does David indicate to us that he had spiritual, physical and psychological afflictions?

b) What was the response of David's friends and companions in his time of need?

c) Discuss and compare the readings from Luke and 2 Chronicles.

DAY 7 The Cry Continues. *Psalm 38:13-22.*

a) How does David express his spiritual anguish?

b) What titles does David use when crying out to God in prayer?

c) How can we experience prayer like David did in (vv. 21 and 22)?

NOTES

Psalm 35

As you read this psalm you will find that David is using some 'strong language' as he asks God to deal with his foes. This is one of several psalms in which the curse of God is requested to fall upon the enemies of David (Ps. 69 is a classic!). They are often called 'Imprecatory Psalms'. When you read phrases like these in the Book of Psalms, when the writer is calling down a curse upon an enemy, it is good to keep the following points in mind:

The writer is not being vindictive.
David repeatedly showed mercy towards those who bitterly hated him.
His prayer is not merely again a personal foe, but against the enemies of God and all His people.

The writer was in mortal danger.
Evil men who would not hesitate to lie, betray, wrongly accuse and even murder were a very real threat to David.

The writer was inspired by God.
The Holy Spirit directed him to write these portions of God's infallible word (2 Tim. 3:16).

The writer lived prior to Christ's incarnation.
He was ignorant of the obligations that Christ has now placed upon his disciples.

Psalm 36

John Bradford, seeing some criminals taken to the gallows exclaimed:
"But for the grace of God, there goes John Bradford."

When we read the first few verses of this psalm, we must realise that the same is true of us. This is man in his natural state, without God.
In contrast, what an incredible picture of God's love is painted in the next verses. As the song goes:

"To write the love of God above would drain the ocean dry,
Nor could the scroll contain the whole,
though stretched from sky to sky."

Psalm 37

10 commandments for freedom from stress:

do not worry	be still
don't be envious	wait patiently for Him
trust in the Lord	do not worry
delight yourself in the Lord	refrain from anger
commit your way to the Lord	do not worry

One of the most puzzling questions for Christians is why people who don't trust in the Lord often seem to prosper and get away with it. But we are told not to let this worry us, God has the answer:

Take a long view, God will judge everyone in his time.

Psalm 38

Try to imagine the condition of this man pouring out his soul to God in these verses. There are many today who can identify with constant pain, crippling disease, depression or guilt.

Do you know anyone like this? Then encourage them to look to God as David did, and perhaps lend them a Christian book on suffering - there are some excellent ones available.

People who are ill need friends who will be sympathetic and positive, not ones who will avoid them as David's friends did.

Dedication: 8. To do your will is my desire.
9. I proclaim righteousness in the great assembly.

STUDY 8

PSALMS 39-42

QUESTIONS

DAY 1 The Brevity of Life. *Psalm 39; James 4:13-16.*

a) James asks, *'What is your life?'* What symbolic descriptions do the psalm writers use to answer the question? See: *(Ps. 78:39; 102:11; 103:15; 144:4).* Life is like a breath, a fleeting shadow. (a wild grass or flower which fades + is blown away quickly).

b) David prayed to God saying, *'Save me from my transgressions.'* Why is it important to personally pray like this?

DAY 2 David's Praise for God's Deliverance. *Psalm 40:1-10; Exodus 21:5, 6; Matthew 5:14-16; Mark 8:38.*

a) Which verses describe David's salvation and which verse his dedication?

Salvation: 2 lifted me out of pit, put me on the rock.
6 my ears you have pierced – I am yours forever.
10. I speak of your faithfulness + salvation.
(13. Be pleased to save me; come quickly to help me)

b) Discuss the importance of sharing our personal experience of God's deliverance with others (see vv. 9-10).

– How else will they know of him as a personal God?

DAY 3 David's Prayer for God's Deliverance. *Psalm 40:11-17; John 9:1-3.*

a) David has physical enemies and outside troubles, but what was the spiritual need for which he asked for deliverance?

vs17 – He is poor + needy
vs12 His sins have overtaken him.

b) In what sense was King David *'poor and needy'*?

His sins have overtaken him – vs12. He needs strength to fight temptation. needs protection from enemies

c) How did Jesus answer the disciples question?

By doing something practical, relating it to the individual. This miracle showed God's glory

DAY 4 Help for those who are Hurt. *Psalm 41:1-6.*

a) What two things is the Lord to be trusted for when we are unwell (v. 3)?

Sustenance + restoration

b) What two things did David ask the Lord for when he was unwell (v. 4)?

Healing + forgiveness

DAY 5 Triumphant despite Trials. *Psalm 41:7-13; John 13:18-30.*

a) Compare David's trial (v. 9) with Christ's experience?

Judas betraying Christ after the passover

b) Discuss our likely reactions in such circumstances?

c) Suggest possible reasons why both David and Christ were triumphant during this particular trial.

They trusted in God.
Prayers

DAY 6 Remembering the Good Time. *Psalm 42:1-5.*

a) What good things in (v. 4), did the psalmist remember prior to feeling downcast?

Worshipping, leading in worship festivals

b) What was the cruel question asked by others?

Where is your God in the midst of suffering?

DAY 7 From being Downcast to Praise. *Psalm 42:6-11.*

a) What was the double question that the psalmist repeated to himself?

VS 5 A why am I downcast?
11 A

b) What did the psalmist say, to indicate that he expected his depression to come to an end?

VS B Put your hope in God for I will yet praise him
V11 B

NOTES

Psalm 39

David reminds himself and us with a variety of poetic expressions that *'Life at best is very brief, like the falling of a leaf.'* It is a sobering thought to consider that we are only one breath away from death and eternity! Or as David once said, *'There is only one step between me and death'* (1 Sam. 20:3).

If life on earth is so short compared with eternity, why am I here? What is the meaning of life? Does it matter how I live?

Some of the most challenging verses in God's word stop us in our tracks and make us think.

"What good is it for a man to gain the whole world, yet forfeit his soul?"
Mark 8:36.

"We brought nothing into this world and we can take nothing out."
1 Timothy 6:7.

"What is seen is temporary, but what is unseen is eternal."
2 Corinthians 4: 18.

We are urged to direct our thoughts to the Lord as David did, and put our hope and trust in Him.

Psalm 40

Do you find it hard to wait patiently? David shows us what God can do when we are willing to wait for Him.

The Holy Spirit inspired David to write prophetically in verses 6-8, and these are quoted in Hebrews 10:5-10, *Therefore, when Christ came into the world, he said: "Sacrifice and offering you did not desire, but a body you prepared for me; with burnt offerings and sin offerings you were not pleased. Then I said, 'Here I am – it is written about me in the scroll - I have come to do your will, O God.' "*

First he said, "Sacrifices and offerings, burnt offerings and sin offerings you did not desire, nor were you pleased with them" (although the law required them to be made).

Then he said, "Here I am, I have come to do your will." He sets aside the first to establish the second. And by that will, we have been made holy through the sacrifice of the body of Jesus Christ once for all.

Jesus spoke these words of himself, showing that the old covenant with its sacrifices of animals was now set aside and that he had come in the human body prepared for him, to offer himself as the one perfect sacrifice.

We can also echo David's words as a prayer: *"I desire to do your will, O my God."*

Psalm 41

Here we have first a picture of a man who is concerned for the weak, the poor, the needy, the sick. Then this man falls ill himself.

Look at the blessings God promises him: God will deliver him, keep him alive, protect him from his enemies, sustain him when he is sick and restore him to health.

Then David finds himself very sick, but God doesn't seem to be meeting his need. David's enemies are having a field day and are just waiting for him to die. Everyone seems to have turned against him, he is not being sustained and he's not getting back his health.

"Lord, don't you desert me," he cries, *"make me well so that I can pay my enemies back!"*(Ps. 41:10 LB)

Having thus cast his burden on the Lord, the God of Israel, he is at peace and can praise Him with joy.

Psalm 42

The imagery of a timid fallow deer audibly panting because it is so thirsty, vividly expresses the longing of the psalmist.

Have you ever felt depressed? The Bible tells us of godly men such as Job, Elijah and David who suffered periods of depression.

The hymn writer, William Cowper (1731 - 1800), who wrote such lines as, "O for a closer walk with God..." and the great pastor and preacher, C.H. Spurgeon, suffered from painful bouts of depression.

This psalm vividly portrays one of God's faithful children passing through gloomy and painful experiences. The writer is struggling with doubts and fears, he longs for a renewed sense of God's presence with him. At the same time he is prepared to challenge himself and in faith look up to God his Saviour. As Spurgeon has so aptly remarked, 'Most of the Lord's family have sailed on the sea which is so graphically described in verse 1.'

STUDY 9

PSALMS 43-46

QUESTIONS

DAY 1 **The Road to Recovery.** *Psalm 43.*

a) What might have been a hindrance to the writer's recovery?

Feelings of rejection + opression

b) What things are mentioned that you consider to have been a help?

Hope, praise.

DAY 2 **'Perplexed, but not in despair.'** *Psalm 44; 2 Corinthians 4:8, 9.*

a) What victories are attributed to God ? (vv. 1-7).

Those which established Israel

b) What encouragement can we receive when downcast?

- Remember God's faithfulness, times when he has rescued us.

DAY 3 **The Divine Bridegroom.** *Psalm 45:1-9.*

a) Link the following texts with verses in the psalm: *Luke 4:22;* V2 *Revelation 1:16; Hebrews 1:8, 9.* V6

b) Who is the Bridegroom that best fits the psalmist's description?

Jesus.

DAY 4 **The Spiritual Bride.** *Psalm 45:10-17; Revelation 19:6-9; Ephesians 5:25, 26, 32.*

a) Who are the spiritual Bride and Bridegroom?

Jesus + the church

b) What is the wedding at which the nations will praise the King for ever and ever?

Heaven

c) Have you responded to your personal invitation to the wedding?

DAY 5 Strength. *Psalm 46:1-3; 2 Corinthians 12:7-9; Isaiah 41:10.*

a) When is strength and help from God especially available?

When we are weak

b) As Believers, why should we not fear our outward circumstances?

nothing can separate us from the Lord

c) Share an experience when you proved God's sufficiency?

DAY 6 Security. *Psalm 46:4-7; Revelation 22:1-5.*

a) What two illustrations does the psalmist use to show the security of the believer?

Refuge strength, Earthquakes, Tidal waves

b) Discuss the presence of the river in the city and its provision?

Central to the city. provides essential water for refreshment, crops, cleaning.

DAY 7 Stillness. *Psalm 46:8-11; 89:9; Mark 4:35-41.*

a) It is difficult to obey the command, *'Be still'* when you are in the midst of a storm. Identify an event in your life when you experienced the Lord's calming power at work?

b) Discuss how we can help others when they are facing storms?

NOTES

Psalm 43

Have you read John Bunyan's *Pilgrim's Progress?* You may remember that Christian sank very easily into the Slough of Despond, but it was difficult getting out even though Help was nearby. Recovery was possible, however, and in this psalm the writer is on the road to recovery after a period of great discouragement.

Take note of the following as the prayer develops:

v. 1 Vindicate me ... rescue me.
v. 2 Why? ... Why?
vv. 3, 4 I will go... I will praise you.
v. 5 Put your hope in God.

Psalm 44

The godly but perplexed writer appears to be speaking for himself and on behalf of God's people. What he says to God could be summarised and paraphrased like this:

> "You have helped, us – You must help us – But, you are not helping us – We are not excluded from being helped because we have done wrong – Therefore, do please help us!"

He certainly sounds perplexed but he is not in despair and neither should we be.

The writer expresses his praise for God's help in the PAST (vv. 1-8), he is rather puzzled about God's dealings in the PRESENT (vv. 9-16), and he appears to be concerned about the FUTURE (vv. 17-26). He sounds just like me at times!

Psalm 45

Imagine this psalm as a wedding cake! It has a silver cake stand (v. 1 – Introduction) and four tiers.

The bottom tier (vv. 2-9) describes the Bridegroom,
the second tier (vv. 10-12) is advice to the Bride,
the third tier (vv. 13-15) shows us the Bride,
and the fourth tier (vv. 16, 17) tells the Bridegroom about the future.

We have seen from New Testament references that Jesus is the one who fulfils the role of the Bridegroom King here.

Even as children we are delighted by stories where the Prince overcomes many difficulties to gain the hand of his Princess whom he loves, and finally marries her and carries her away to his castle. Even Cinderella is lifted from her cinders to become the bride of her Prince.

How wonderful that we are part of the Bride of Christ and will go to be with Him in His home. And this is one story where it will be true to say: 'They lived happily ... ever after!'

Psalm 46

Noise and turbulence is contrasted with peace and stability in this striking psalm.

Earth gives way, mountains quake and fall, seas roar, BUT God is our refuge.

Nations are in uproar, kingdoms fall, BUT God is in his holy city.

Desolations come on the earth, God shatters the instruments of war, BUT God is our fortress.

The 'chorus' in verses 7 and 11 contains three titles for God:

1. The Lord Almighty (the Lord of hosts) shows his divine power.

2. The God of Jacob is his title of covenant relationship.

3. God is with us, his name is Immanuel.

STUDY 10

PSALMS 47-50

QUESTIONS

DAY 1 The Universal King. *Psalms 47; Hebrews 12:28; 13:15.*

a) List the phrases used in the psalm that clearly indicate that the Lord is not a 'national' but the 'universal' King.

b) How should we worship, if Christ is King over our lives?

DAY 2 The City of God. *Psalm 48; Revelation 21:1, 2, 22-27.*

a) Which verses in the psalm tell us about the city's Sovereign? Which speak of its security and which invite us to survey 'her'?

b) What activity is described as taking place in God's temple? In which city was no temple seen?

c) When did God write your name in the Book of the Living?

DAY 3 A Proverb about Prosperity. *Psalm 49:1-15; 1 Peter 1:18-21, 24, 25.*

a) Suggest things that money cannot buy.

b) Discuss the significance of verses 7-9 and 15. Compare them with 1 Peter 1:18-21.

DAY 4 Wise Words about Wealth. *Psalm 49:16-20; Job 1:20, 21; 1 Timothy 6:7; Matthew 6:19-21.*

a) What is the sober reminder about wealth in these texts?:

b) What is Christ's antidote to the love of money?

Store up treasures in Heaven

c) What treasure controls my heart?

DAY 5 A Divine Summons. *Psalm 50:1-6; Isaiah 1:2; Hebrews 10:30, 31.*

a) What was it that prompted God to make such a far reaching summons? Note *verse 1-4*. Compare *Isaiah 1:2* and *Hebrews 10:30-31.*

b) What event could verse 3 be applied to? Compare 2 Peter 3:10-13.

DAY 6 A Divine Speech. *Psalm 50:7-23; 1 Peter 4:17.*

a) What does God want his people to do? *(vv. 14, 15, 23)*.

b) In what respect were the wicked like God's people? *(vv. 16-21)*.

c) What challenge comes to us from *1 Peter 4:17*.

DAY 7 Review and Reflect. *Psalms 2:7-9; 22:1-18; 24:7-10; 45:1-9.* Many of the psalms are prophetic and refer to the Lord Jesus Christ.

a) Which psalm speaks of Christ's suffering on the cross, his universal conquest, likens him to being a Bridegroom, and as being the King of Glory?

NOTES

Psalm 47

Is heaven going to be a quiet place?

In Revelation the praise in heaven is described as *"the roar of rushing waters and like loud peals of thunder"* (Rev. 19:6) as ten thousand times ten thousand angels and a multitude of the redeemed sing:

> *"Hallelujah! The Lord God Almighty reigns."*

It is no wonder, then, that we are told in this psalm to clap our hands, shout to God, give shouts of joy as the trumpets are sounded! We on earth sing the same song:

> *"Praise to God! (Hallelujah) God reigns over all the earth."*

What an exciting psalm! You can just imagine the director of music getting together all the musicians and singers, and making a wonderfully joyful noise.

Psalm 48

The main topic of the song is, *"The city of our God"*, *"the city of the Great King"*, *"the city of the Lord Almighty"*.

The New Testament sheds more helpful light on this subject. We are informed that Abraham *"was looking forward to the city with foundations, whose architect and builder is God"* (Heb. 11:10). The writer also tells us that those who had been living by faith *"were longing for a better country – a heavenly one"* and that God *"has prepared a city for them"* (Heb. 11:15-16).

The writer then goes on to say that they *"have come to Mount Zion to the heavenly Jerusalem, the city of the living God."*

In a vision, the Apostle John saw *"the holy City, the new Jerusalem, coming down out of heaven from God, prepared as a bride beautifully dressed for her husband"* (Rev. 21:2). From such relevant passages we can conclude that a spiritual application of the city can be made. The 'city' spoken of in the psalm is an instructive illustration of the glory of the true church of God, 'the city of the living God'.

Did you notice verse 14? This is a good one to write out and look at often.
For this God is our God for ever and ever; he will be our guide even to the end.

Psalm 49

What an important and practical matter is now dealt with by the writer of the psalm.

From the outset we are all summoned to listen and learn. No matter how we might classify ourselves, high or low, rich or poor, this is the word of the Lord for us. We need to give our attention to the possible effects of worldly wealth upon our lives. This is because prosperity can be a hazardous problem.

"The love of money is the root of all kinds of evil" the Apostle Paul warns us in (1 Tim. 6:10). *"It is easier for a camel to go through the eye of a needle than for a rich man to enter the kingdom of God declared the Saviour"* (Matt. 19:24). Material prosperity can lead us into a multitude of temptations, such as jealousy, greed, covetousness and idolatry. Some have even murdered for the sake of money! We cannot afford to ignore the warnings that God has given to us in His Word about such perils.

Psalm 50

The setting here is a great Courtroom, where God sits as Judge. He summons heaven and earth as witnesses to His righteousness, and the case proceeds.

First in the dock:	His covenant people.
The charge:	though they have performed their ritual duties regularly, their motives have been wrong. They thought God needed these sacrificial beasts and that He should be grateful to them. What nonsense!
His advice:	True worship does not consist in offering up dead beasts, but in the personal response of thanksgiving and faithfulness to God.
His promise:	*"Call upon Me... I will deliver you."*
Next in the dock:	the wicked.
The charge:	They have been hypocrites, knowing the laws but not keeping them. He lists their serious offences.
The sentence:	God's rebuke, accusation and terrible wrath.
His offer:	Salvation to any who repent and obey Him.

In what ways did David ask God for help and protection?

ANSWER GUIDE

The following pages are only a guide to the questions asked and are in no way exhaustive. To get the full benefit from these studies, it is recommended that you answer the questions first before turning to the answer guide. Remember to read through the notes again after completing your study.

GUIDE TO STUDY 1

DAY 1 a) The saint, the godly person, the righteous. The sinner, the ungodly, the wicked.
b) Personal.

DAY 2 a) 'Anointed One' = Messiah (Hebrew) and Christ (Greek). King (Compare *Rev. 19:16*).
b) Nations, peoples, kings, rulers - many from various backgrounds. To laugh, rebuke and install my king.

DAY 3 a) Son. To all nations, to 'the ends of the earth'.
b) The need to love Christ ('kiss the Son'), to avoid God's wrath.
c) There is real happiness ('blessed'), for those who seek spiritual safety in Christ.

DAY 4 a) Personal.
b) Prayer, the Lord sustaining him.

DAY 5 a) God answers our prayer.
b) Complete trust in the Lord.

DAY 6 a) Praying and listening.
b) Personal.
c) That they will 'be glad', 'sing for joy' and 'rejoice' in the Lord.

DAY 7 a) Godly.
b) No. We need also to pray for God's mercy *(Luke 18:13)*, ask God for forgiveness and have faith in Christ. *(Eph. 2:8)*.

Weeping will not save me!
Though my face were bathed in tears,
That could not allay my fears;
Could not wash the sins of years
Weeping will not save me.

GUIDE TO STUDY 2

DAY 1 a) He prayed for deliverance and for justice to be done.
b) It was said earnestly. There was submission to God and a personal relationship with him.

DAY 2 a) Personal.
b) God will judge them and lets trouble recoil upon them (vv. 11-14).

DAY 3 a) The Lord Jesus Christ.
b) Issues arising from such matters as euthanasia, care of sick and dying, war, assault, evolutionary theories, racialism, abortion etc. may be relevant.

DAY 4 a) (vv. 1-2), worship; testimony, living a joyful life, singing praises.
b) (vv. 3-6), The fact that justice is done is a good reason for praising the Lord. God does not take delight in the death of the wicked, their final judgement brings honour and glory to God who keeps His Word.
c) Personal.

DAY 5 a) See phrases used in verses 2 and 7-12. The ungodly should be fearful, and the godly thankful.

DAY 6 a) Human weakness, sin, lack of trust, difficult circumstances.
b) God knows about our trials. He does consider our need and is willing to help. Compare *Exodus 3:7-8.*

DAY 7 a) Personal.

GUIDE TO STUDY 3

DAY 1 a) Lies, flattering lips, to freely strut about and what is vile is honoured, (vv 2, 8).
b) Personal (may / all).
c) Trust the Lord and pray.

DAY 2 a) Personal.
b) When David meditated upon God's constant goodness, he sang praises to him.

DAY 3 a) A fool for Christ.
b) Examples could include the foolish builder *(Matt. 7:26, 27)*, the parable of the foolish virgins *(Matt. 25:1-13)*, and the rich fool *(Luke 12:16-20)*.

DAY 4 a) Eleven.
b) Personal
c) Those 'whose walk is blameless'. True believers, who make up the Kingdom of God.

DAY 5 a) Faith in God.
b) Peter and Paul apply the words to Christ.

DAY 6 a) Confess our sins.
b) Personal.

DAY 7 a) Keep me, hide me, rescue me, save me from the wicked. Pray that I may be rescued from unbelievers in Judea.
b) Each share a prayer request and pray for each other before closing.

GUIDE TO STUDY 4

DAY 1 a) David's very personal and close relationship with the Lord.
b) Personal but be willing to discuss.

DAY 2 a) The Lord *(v. 28)*.
b) David *(v. 35)*.
c) David's enemies *(vv. 40-41)*.

DAY 3 a) Mankind is without an excuse about God's existence. He is seen through creation.
b) A time to share *(vv. 7-11)*.

DAY 4 a) Personal.
b) *Verses* 5-6.
c) Local and national leaders of state and church.

DAY 5 a) Personal.
b) At the time of Christ's 'appearing', that is, at His return, it will be a fearful time of judgement for the unconverted. Compare *Revelation* 20:11-15.

DAY 6 a) Complaining: *(vv. 1-2, 6-8, 12-18)*.
b) Trusting: *(vv. 3-5, 9-11, 19-21)*.
c) Personal.

DAY 7 a) When we repent and believe. When we personally trust Christ as Lord and Saviour.
b) Suggestion - recite the psalm as a group.

GUIDE TO STUDY 5

DAY 1 a) Holiness in every aspect of our being *(v. 4)*.
b) All who believe on the Lord Jesus Christ.

DAY 2 a) Personal.
b) The Lord his God.
c) Show me your ways, teach me your paths. Give me guidance, deliverance forgiveness; teach me how to live.

DAY 3 a) God the Holy Spirit often uses the written and preached Word of God to convict and awaken our conscience; so that we are aware of the issues that displease the Lord.
b) 'I will praise the Lord.'

DAY 4 a) Personal faith in the Lord and trust in His Word.
b) Personal.

DAY 5 a) Various possibilities, including the Lord's guidance and protection.
b) 'Wait for the Lord, - Trust in the Lord'.

DAY 6 a) We need personal holiness and a right attitude towards others as we gather for prayer.
b) He gives me joy and makes me glad.

DAY 7 a) Ascribing glory to God and worshipping him.
b) He is powerful, majestic, awesome, authoritative, etc.

GUIDE TO STUDY 6

DAY 1 a) Personal.
b) The Lord his God.
c) To give God 'thanks for ever'.

DAY 2 a) They all passed through periods of great stress. *(vv. 1-3, 5a, 6, 13)*.
b) A refuge, a defence, a faithful God whose love is constant.

DAY 3 a) 'I am cut off from your sight!' *(v. 22)*.
b) Personal.
c) He could testify to God's goodness, praise God for his love and encourage others to hope in the Lord (*2 Cor. 1:4*).

DAY 4 a) See *(vv. 4-5)*.
b) He was assured of God's forgiveness, protection and guidance.
c) The righteous, the upright in heart *(v. 11)*.

DAY 5 a) The evolutionist's theories of unbelievers stand in complete contrast to the Biblical account of creation: *Genesis 1–2; Hebrews 1:10; 11:3*.

b) Several possible reasons including: It is a repeated Biblical exhortation. It glorifies the Lord. It is a good witness to the unconverted.

DAY 6 a) Add applicable examples. A Christian marriage proposal; an exhortation at the beginning of a service; a personal word of encouragement.
b) He praised God, acknowledged God's answer to his prayer, testified openly and encouraged others to praise God with him.
c) Angels, extolled and glorified.

DAY 7 a) See *verses 15-17.*
b) There is no condemnation (judgement in hell) for believers.
c) *No-one will be condemned who takes refuge in him. Therefore, there is now no condemnation for those who are in Christ Jesus.*

GUIDE TO STUDY 7

DAY 1 a) The angel of the Lord helps to protect God's people against the attack of the enemy, and executes judgement when necessary.
b) David requested a curse; Christ commanded that the Christian's enemies should be loved and prayed for.

DAY 2 a) Nathan, Christ, Stephen and Paul.
b) They loved God and sought to please and obey him.
c) Personal.

DAY 3 a) Sinful, wicked, unrighteous, deceitful, foolish,
b) 'No fear of God before their eyes'.
c) Love, faithfulness, righteousness, justice.

DAY 4 a) Personal.
b) Personal.

DAY 5 a) Removed, destroyed (judged), cut off. A future (life), salvation, deliverance.
b) Personal.

DAY 6 a) He speaks about his sin, guilt and sinful folly *(vv. 3 -5).* No health in his body *(vv. 3, 7).* He moaned and groaned in anguish of heart *(vv. 6, 8).*
b) They avoid him and stay far away.
c) Personal.

DAY 7 a) See *(v. 8).*
b) Lord, my God, my Saviour. Denotes submission, a personal relationship, and faith in God to help and save.
c) By coming to a personal belief in the Lord Jesus Christ.

GUIDE TO STUDY 8

DAY 1 a) A passing breeze. An evening shadow, grass. Grass, flower of the field. A breath, a fleeting shadow.
b) All have sinned, all need God's forgiveness. We only have this life in which to prepare for eternity. God holds us responsible to confess our own sin.

DAY 2 a) *Verses 1, 3, 5, 6-8*. (compare *Exod. 21:5-6*).
b) It brings glory to God, helps and blesses others and stimulates our own faith and courage.

DAY 3 a) His sins (*v. 12*).
b) Spiritually and physically, he needed protection from his foes.
c) Neither this man or his parents sinned but this was done for the glory of God. This miracle displayed the work of God in his life.

DAY 4 a) To sustain and restore.
b) God's mercy (forgiveness) and healing.

DAY 5 a) Personal.
b) Prayer and remaining fully dependent upon God for help and strength.

DAY 6 a) See *verse 4*.
b) 'Where is your God?' (*v. 3*).

DAY 7 a) *'Why are you downcast, O my soul? Why so disturbed within me?'* (*vv. 5, 11*).
b) *'I will yet praise him, my Saviour and my God.'* (*vv. 5, 11*).

GUIDE TO STUDY 9

DAY 1 a) He prayed, trusted the Lord and looked forward to a time of joyful praise and worship.
b) He asked questions that God may not have answered.

DAY 2 a) Power, strength, assurance of God's presence .
b) Not crushed, never in despair, never without a friend, not destroyed.

DAY 3 a) Psalm 45:2, 3, 6 and 7.
b) The Lord Jesus Christ.

DAY 4 a) Christ and his Church.
b) The Wedding of the Lamb.
c) Personal.

DAY 5 a) When we are weak and in trouble.
b) Outward circumstances are temporary; we have an eternal security in the Lord.

DAY 6 a) A city and a fortress.
b) All that is required for life is provided within the security of the city. Gladness, joy, refreshment, security, healing.

DAY 7 a) Personal.

GUIDE TO STUDY 10

DAY 1 a) 'King over all the earth' *(v. 2)*; 'King of all the earth' *(v. 7)*. 'God reigns over the nations' *(v. 8)*; 'Kings of the earth belong to God'(v. 9).
b) Thankfully, acceptably with reverence and awe, with joyful praise, etc.

DAY 2 a) The city's Sovereign - *(vv. 1-2)*, its security - *(vv. 3, 8)*, the invitation to survey *(vv. 12-13)*.
b) Meditation of God's unfailing love. The Holy City, the new Jerusalem – heaven.
c) Personal.

DAY 3 a) Such things as health, lasting happiness and salvation.
b) Our redemption is a personal matter; only the Lord can redeem our lives; it cannot be acquired by the payment of money, or by living good lives.

DAY 4 a) All material things are left behind when we die.
b) Storing up treasures in heaven.
c) Personal.

DAY 5 a) The offensive sin of those who declared themselves to be God's people. God's final summons Christ's return and the day of judgement.

DAY 6 a) Thankfulness, worship, fulfil your promises, call to him, praise him.
b) They recited God's law and spoke of his covenant. God held them accountable, and rebuked them for their sin. Personal.

DAY 7 a) *Psalm 22:7-9;* Christ's suffering on the cross. *Psalm 2:8;* His universal conquest. *Psalm 45:2, 7, 8;* Dressed as a bridegroom, anointed and beautifully robed. *Psalm 24:7-10;* The King of glory.

GEARED FOR GROWTH BIBLE STUDIES

Enable you to:

1. Have a daily encounter with God
2. Encourage you to apply the Word of God to everyday life
3. Help you to share your faith with others
4. They are straightforward, practical, non-controversial and inexpensive.

WEC INTERNATIONAL is involved in gospel outreach, church planting and discipleship training using every possible means including radio, literature, medical work, rural development schemes, correspondence courses and telephone counselling. Nearly two thousand workers are involved in their fields and sending bases.

Find out more from the following Website:
www.wec-int.org.uk

A full list of over 50 'Geared for Growth' studies can be obtained from:

UK GEARED FOR GROWTH COORDINATORS

John and Ann Edwards
8, Sidings Terrace, Skewen, Neath, W.Glam, SA10 6RE
Email: rhysjohn.edwards@virgin.net
Tel. 01792 814994

UK Website: www.gearedforgrowth.co.uk

For information on Geared for Growth Bible Studies in other languages contact:

Word Worldwide International Coordinators
Kip and Doreen Wear
Tel. 01269 870842
Email: kip.wear@virgin.net

Christian Focus Publications

Publishes books for all ages

Our mission statement –
STAYING FAITHFUL
In dependence upon God we seek to help make His infallible word, the Bible, relevant. Our aim is to ensure that the Lord Jesus Christ is presented as the only hope to obtain forgiveness of sin, live a useful life and look forward to heaven with Him.
REACHING OUT
Christ's last command requires us to reach out to our world with His gospel. We seek to help fulfil that by publishing books that point people towards Jesus and help them to develop a Christ-like maturity. We aim to equip all levels of readers for life, work, ministry and mission.

Books in our adult range are published in three imprints.

Christian Focus contains popular works including biographies, commentaries, basic doctrine, and Christian living. Our children's books are published in this imprint.

Mentor focuses on books written at a level suitable for Bible College and seminary students, pastors, and other serious readers. The imprint includes commentaries, doctrinal studies, examination of current issues, and church history.

Christian Heritage contains classic writings from the past.

For details of our titles visit us on our website
www.christianfocus.com

ISBN 978-1-84550-408-3

Published in 2008 by
Christian Focus Publications,
Geanies House, Fearn, Ross-shire,
IV20 1TW, Scotland
and
WEC International,
Bulstrode, Oxford Road,
Gerrards Cross, Bucks, SL9 8SZ

Cover design by Alister MacInnes
Printed by Bell & Bain, Glasgow